Space Observer

SPACE TRAVEL

Jenny Tesar

Heinemann
LIBRARY

First published in Great Britain by Heinemann Library
Halley Court, Jordan Hill, Oxford OX2 8EJ
a division of Reed Educational and Professional Publishing Ltd.

Heinemann is a registered trademark of Reed Educational & Professional Publishing Limited.

OXFORD   MELBOURNE   AUCKLAND
JOHANNESBURG   BLANTYRE   GABORONE
IBADAN   PORTSMOUTH NH   CHICAGO

Designed by AMR and Celia Floyd
Originated by Dot Gradations Ltd
Printed and bound in Hong Kong/China

04 03 02 01 00
10 9 8 7 6 5 4 3 2 1

ISBN 0 431 01443 4

British Library Cataloguing in Publication Data

Tesar, Jenny
  Space Travel. – (Space observer) (Take-off!)
  1. Interplanetary voyages – Juvenile literature 2. Space
  flight – Juvenile literature
  I. Title
  387.8

Acknowledgements

The publishers would like to thank the following for permission to reproduce photographs:
Pages 4–5, 5 (inset), 6, 10–11, 13, 14, 15, 16–17, 20–21: Photri; pages 7, 12, 14, 18: ©NASA; pages 8, 9, 19: Gazelle
Technologies, Inc.; pages 22-23: A. Gragera, Latin Stock/Science Photo Library/Photo Researchers, Inc.

Cover photograph: The Stock Market/Mark M. Lawrence

The Publishers would like to thank Sue Graves and Stephanie Byars for their advice and expertise in the
preparation of this book.

Every effort has been made to contact copyright holders of any material reproduced in this book.
Any omissions will be rectified in subsequent printings if notice is given to the Publisher.

For more information about Heinemann Library books, or to order, please telephone +44(0)1865 888066, or send
a fax to +44(0)1865 314091. You can visit our website at www.heinemann.co.uk

Any words appearing in bold, **like this**, are explained in the Glossary.

Contents

Going into space

For thousands of years people have always dreamed of going into space.

The first person to travel into space was a Russian called Yuri Gagarin. He went into space in 1961. He made one complete **orbit** of the Earth before landing again. He was in space for only 108 minutes. Since then hundreds of people have travelled into space. Some have even walked on the Moon.

Yuri Gagarin's spaceship was called *Vostok 1*.

Russian **astronaut**
Yuri Gagarin.

Mission control

A space trip is called a mission. It is controlled by people on the ground in a place called mission control. People use **radio signals** and computers to contact the spaceship.

This mission control is at the Kennedy Space Centre in America.

This astronaut is being trained at mission control.

Astronauts are specially trained by the people at mission control. The astronauts learn how to wear space suits, move about and work in space, and operate their spaceships.

Leaving Earth

Spaceships have to be very powerful to escape Earth's **atmosphere**. The spaceships get their energy from big, powerful rockets. Spaceships are attached to rockets so they can be **launched** into space.

Rockets help the spaceship take off.

This spaceship is heading for space.

To get a spaceship into **orbit** it must travel at 8km a second! If it doesn't travel at that speed, the spaceship will fall back to Earth.

To get a spaceship to the Moon it must travel at 11 km a second!

Space shuttle

A space **shuttle** is a small spaceship that travels back and forth between Earth and space.

Space shuttles carry **astronauts** and materials into space. The astronauts do tests to learn how space affects their bodies. They fix damaged **satellites**. They also study Earth and other objects in space.

Two astronauts work in space. They are connected to their shuttle by strong attachments so that they do not float off into space.

Living in space

Space is very different from Earth. In space there is no food, air or water. It is important that the spaceships carry all these things for the **astronauts**. Without them, people could not live in space.

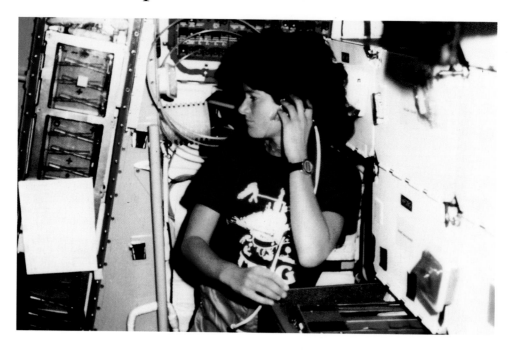

An astronaut, in space, talks with mission control.

A spacesuit protects the astronaut from the heat and cold in space.

Spacesuits protect astronauts from the very hot and very cold temperatures in space.

Just one spacesuit can cost millions of pounds!

Working in space

Inside the spaceship, the temperature is controlled. This means that it is not too hot or too cold. **Astronauts** can wear light, comfortable clothes when they are working inside the spaceship.

This astronaut wears light clothes in the spaceship.

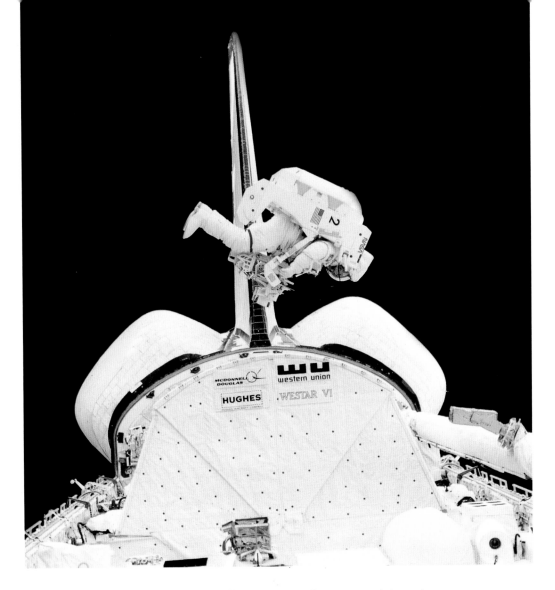

This astronaut wears a spacesuit when working in space.

Outside the spaceship astronauts wear special spacesuits. A spacesuit contains air to breathe and earphones and a microphone so the astronauts can talk to each other.

Space stations

A space station is a kind of **satellite**. It is a place where **astronauts** can live in space. Spaceships bring astronauts and also supplies, such as food and water, to a space station.

In 1996, an American woman called Shannon Lucid lived in the Russian space station, *Mir*, for more than six months. She travelled 120 million kilometres and circled Earth 3008 times!

Shannon Lucid works with another astronaut at the *Mir* space station.

Moon landings

American **astronauts** Neil Armstrong and Buzz Aldrin were the first people to walk on the Moon. They landed their **spacecraft**, *Apollo 11,* on the Moon on July 20, 1969.

Buzz Aldrin was the second man to step onto the Moon, after Neil Armstrong.

An astronaut collects rock samples from the Moon.

There were five more Moon landings after *Apollo 11*. The astronauts collected rock samples to take back to Earth for testing.

Space probes

Space probes are **unmanned spacecraft** that explore outer space. Probes carry cameras, **radar**, and other instruments. They send information back to Earth.

Space probes have taken photos that scientists can use to make maps of space. In 1997, a space probe landed on Mars to find out more about the planet.

This is an artist's drawing of the space probe *Voyager 2* near Neptune and one of its moons.

Space colonies

In the future, people may be able to live on different **planets**. They may live in places called space **colonies**. The space colonies would have homes, schools and farms. These colonies would have to be built under big domes filled with air.

Will you become a space person?

This imaginary space base could grow to be a space colony!

Glossary

astronauts people who travel to space

atmosphere mixture of gases around a planet

colonies communities of people who have left their home country to settle in a new place

launched sent into space

orbit path around the Sun or around another object in space

planet one of nine huge, ball-shaped objects that circle the Sun

radar equipment that uses radio waves to find solid objects

radio signals a wave of energy used to send information

satellite a spacecraft that travels in a path in space

shuttle something that moves back and forth from one place to another

spacecraft a vehicle that travels to space

unmanned without people

Index